THE MAJESTIC DREAMSCAPE

A POETRY COMPILATION

NAMASKRITA RAO

To you, dear reader, who breathes life into these pages.

"Every Phase In Our Life

Is Bound To Teach Us

Something Valueable

But It Depends On Us

Whether We Ananlyse The Lesson

Or Turn The Pages"

- Dr.R.P Chadha

Contents

Foreword

The book "The Majestic Dreamscape" is a poetry compilation consisting of poems written by a 14 year old over a peiod of long years. The author Namaskrita Rao is a teenager who believes that dreaming is a right given to each and every individual irrespective of their physical or mental characteristics. The way I express the words consists of emotions that are very well capable of describing a dream. I loved to write poetries and short stories since I was 8 years old. I was obsessed with writing short horror and suspense stories. But one day, a topic seized my attention..Dreams.

What are Dreams? It is not something that you see when you're asleep. It is something that doesn't let you sleep. The teenager that was slumbered within me woke up one day and made me reconsider my abstraction. Since that day on, I started writing poetries about dreams and what we lost. The world we're staying in is nothing without dreams. If one day a person had never thought.. or I should say dreamed about making a mobile phone.. would we have it right now? no. Dream is the beginning of a series of sucessful events.

"Every great dream begins with a dreamer. Always remember you have within you the strength, the patience, and the passion to reach for the stars to change the world."

Preface

The Majestic Dreamscape" consists of poetries about Dreams. All the poems in this book have a connection with the real world in one or other means. This book also consists of the meaning of every poem followed by the poetic matter. A real world is nothing without dreams. All of my thoughts have been collected, reconsidered and modified which resulted in bringing this book into being.

I have always been interested in writing poetries and short stories. But this time, I decided to share my views and thoughts with the world. This book consists of 13 poetries followed by their meanings. I always wondered what the world would've looked if dreams were phantasmic. The characters and stories that we see in our dreams are definitely phantasmagoric, but the ideas shared aren't.

"A dream doesn't become reality through magic; it takes sweat, determination and hardwork."

Acknowledgements

I would like to acknowledge and give my warmest thanks to my reader who made this journey worthwhile. Thank you so much for investing your time and reading my poetries.

Special Thanks to my parents, Subrata Rao and Rakhi Rao, who supported me and gave me the required guidance and advices. I could not have done this accomplishment in such an early age without their support.

Thank you so much to my friends for helping and designing the book. Your guidance and advice made it possible for me to publish my book.

You need people in your life who support and guide you, not make you feel unworthy and useless. These are the people who made me feel worthy and helped me publish my book..

"The Majestic Dreamscape."

Thank you so much.

1. The Light Beam

*I was **idiosyncratic**,*

*But they called me **peculiar***

*I was told to visit a **psychiatrist**, But I chose to call them a **liar***

*I was meant for **bonanza,** but they let it all **go***

*I would've been reading a **stanza,** but they've found me a **row***

*As I lay myself on the **comforting seat***

*I feel my adroitness grow **weak***

*I had dreams of becoming a **writer***

*But they shoo 'ed it away like a **fighter***

*I **perceived**; I was not meant **here**.*

*My **place**, the stage was waiting up **there***

*I went there to speak my **heartout***

*And what I received was a **greatshout out***

*This taught me to never pretermit my **dreams***

*As I stood there as **brilliant as ever***

like a shining light beam

The Light Beam

Meaning

'The Light Beam' is a poetry based on the feelings of a writer... who thought of giving up many times because of social stereotypes and discriminations. In this poem the word 'They' is referred to as the people who hated you or did not support you on your way up.

The only way to achieve success is not listening to the negligence. Never ever give up on your dreams, instead create a circle of good people who support you.

When people meet someone whose thoughts and views are different from other's perceptions, then people most likely hate or despise them. It is a common human nature. But we, as an individual who craves success have to ignore their words and keep on growing and nurturing ourselves.

2. The Veracity Of Conurbation

We all have been through the honour of nature
But no one has ever seen the beauty of the nature
We live here in a city filled with hush
Where people are always in a rush
I stay in hurry
While the nature stays in fury
I was sitting with misery
But the nature observed me flawlessly
But I was in a hurry
While nature showed its fury

The Veracity Of Conurbation

Meaning

'The Veracity Of Conurbation' is a poetry based on the beauty of nature. It is so unfortunate that we all are stuck up here living a busy life, whereas the nature must be waiting for us to play with it, observe it, and relax within its lap. We all stay in hurry which makes the nature stay in fury. This is what we call unfortune. The nature has hidden treasure for us which we can unravel by the never-ending curiosity and vision in our mind.

Urban life is not easy. And especially with the rapid growth of development we forget to see what's more important to us. Nature hides so much within its lap but we fail to see it due to the concrete walls we hide behind.

Make sure to appreciate the nature and preserve every ounce of beauty it holds.

3. The 'IT' Girl

You see me, as the girl

Who is fearless

You see me, as the girl

Who is painless

You see me, as the girl

Who has magic in her every verse

But do you see the real me?

The real me having pain

The real me having no gain

The real me always worrying for name and fame

Wow! Such a shame

I don't remind myself that

I am an item to be framed.

The 'IT' Girl

Meaning

This poem describes the truth of how humans feel nowadays. There are unrealistic standards that are set up in order to be 'popular' or 'perfect'. How dumb it is for us humans to forget the human nature of ourselves. In search of gold, we lost diamonds. We lost so many individuals who lost their lives just because of these unrealistic standards.

In this poem, there's a girl who states how fake she has to be just so that the society likes her. She has to hold her despondency and put up a tough character. But there will be a time when you will grow up enough to value your own life. I feel proud to realise that those standards are fake. Please, realise that you are an item to be frames, in the sense, you are so capable, able-bodied, precious and unique that you should be preserved.

Humanity is not putting others down, it is growing up to learn that you are blessed to be a human.

4. Alienation Ahead

In the world,

Where I stand

My dreams have no chance

I see my vision burst

As I notice the divisions manifest the world

The divvying up is causing me to feel alienated

Causing me to feel devastated

I can just imagine

How virtue the world would've been

If there was no division causing to break the dream.

Alienation Ahead

Meaning

We have seen ants circling up in a specific border. Beneath that, no ant dares to move. Aren't we humans the same? Living inside the border of our countries... and fighting with our brothers?

The divvying up is causing our further generations to normalize loneliness and feel that their lives are better off alone. People support being superior to one another while side lining the fact that unity is strength.

For example, there are 100 red ants and 100 black ants locked up in a jar. Nothing will happen. But if a person shakes the jar, then the ants will starts killing each other. The black ants will think that the red ones are the enemy, whereas the red ones will think that the black ones are the enemy. The same thing happens in our society. People are busy fighting with each other and divvying up this diverse society. They think that they themselves are their enemies, but the real enemy is the person who shook the jar. We need to find out who shook the jar?

There's no reason in hating each other and proving that they are inferior to you. Instead, let us become a single unit and lean forward towards the development of humanity.

5. The Acrimony

There comes a competition

Where everyone is set upon a mission

Half of them are trying to establish their supremacies

Half of them are just trying to keep up with the joneses

Everyone wants to procure triumph

Everyone wants to be the king lion

But someone wants to just carry the day

After long hours of packing the hay

They understand that competition is not going to help them in

their way

But only the hard work and the determination will pay.

The Acrimony

Meaning

Being the winner, seems like such a convincing and applaudable idea. We have so many people who want to bag that *1st position... Yes, that 1st position.* We all crave for the attention, recognition and respect the winner gets. It is basic human nature to desire for such things. We even get dozens of people coming to comfort us in such situations but there's a wise statement... *Everybody that you fight is not your enemy and everybody that helps you is not your friend.* We live in a society where superiority matters and people are crazy for this.

But these competitions are only for the rich ones, aren't they? The poor ones have much more to do in their life. There's a difference between being rich and wealthy. *Rich is loud... Wealth is powerful.* The real wealth of our nation are our farmers, the people who work hard just to feed the rich who are sitting and considering themselves 'wealthy'. Lion is not the biggest animal, neither the strongest, not the tallest... but still it is the king. In our society, Peasants are not the richest, neither the wealthiest, nor the healthiest... but we, normal beings cannot live without them, can we? They are not a part of the competition, yet they come first. They are the primary producers. Similarly, let us be our primary producers and be independent in all sorts of way possible. Try to be *wealthy* not *rich.*

6. Vainglory

Every part of YOU is unique
Your eye shows the truth
Your mouth shows the kindness
Your mind shows the wisdom
Your hand shows the travail
Your foot shows the path
But.. What do they show?
Negligence? Fiasco? Dissent-ness?

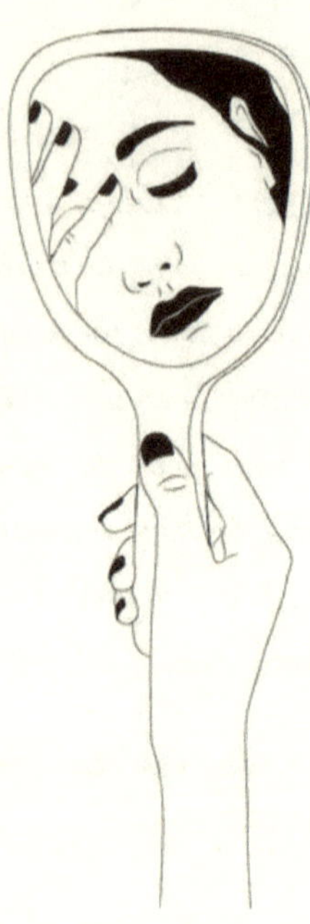

Vainglory

Meaning

Vainglory is a term defined as inordinate or unwarranted pride in one's accomplishments or qualities. In common language, we call it 'ego'. Humans nowadays have a tendency to regenerate their worth. People look for validation instead of accomplishing their goals. We forget how strong we mankind are..

If someone tells a lie, smart ones find the truth out just by seeing their eyes.

If one speaks, their kindness is withdrawn from their heart.

If one thinks, their intelligence is showcased.

If one works hard, their hands will portray it.

If one travels in search of success, their footprints will show their struggle.

We have so many hidden characteristics which can make us feel proud. People have mistaken self-confidence with ego. Ego is not equal to self-confidence. Ego is a totally different psychological concept whereas self-confidence is a mindset that each and every human should inhibit.

Remember, Attitude is a small thing, that makes a huge difference.

7. Ignored Incivility

When they disrespect you
With their attitude
Show them your quietude
No wonder they will enjoy
But your tranquillity will bring you endless joy.

Ignored Incivility

Meaning

People disrespect me, people disrespect you, people disrespect him, people disrespect her and everyone that you can ever imagine. Sometimes you have to act like a fool to fool those fools who think you are a fool. Twisty enough, but it's true. People will have opinion. That's their priority in their work-less life. You, as a smart individual should know the proper response to their disrespect. The biggest response you can give them is, by distancing yourself from such people for a period of time until they realise your significance.

Well-educated people know that disrespecting someone is not a sign of strength, it is a display of one's insecurity. We should keep a habit of forgiving others and giving them a chance to secure their insecurity, shouldn't we? Forgiving people can help us free from the control of the people who harmed us. Silence is the best response to disrespect. Let the opponent realise their mistake and mishap. And if they don't realise, it is time to wave them off. Remember, Silence is Power.

8. My Merit

A butterfly doesn't need to be told it's beautiful
A Lamborghini doesn't need to be told it's expensive
A superhero doesn't need to be told he's powerful
A pen doesn't need to be told it's useful
A kind person doesn't need to be told he's kind
It just is.

My Merit

Meaning

It's a tendency of mankind to seek for validation and vindication. People continuously ask for validation just to prove themselves. In our society, we have thousands of influencers who help the poor population and post it on social networking platforms. I clearly don't understand, if you're doing a good deed, do it for yourself, do it for the person in need! What is the need to show it off all over the internet?

In the teenage years, a person's brain is still developing and hence they are still unsure about their capabilities and responsibilities. Adolescents ask for validation the most. They want to be loved and hear the things that they long for. 'My Merit' is a poem which describes that one doesn't need validation to be significant. A butterfly is beautiful indeed. And the butterfly knows it. A Lamborghini driver doesn't need to be told that his car is expensive. He knows it. Similarly, A kind person doesn't need to be told that he's kind. If you keep on nagging a person to do some good deed and then he does it, that's not kindness... A person doing good deeds just because it's his nature... That is called kindness.

9. The Nirvanic Poet

When I look out of the window,
I see children playing
Said the teacher
When I look out of the window,
I see a good land
Said the landlord
When I look out of the window,
I see blooming flowers
Said the florist
When I look out of the window,
I see nirvana
Said the poet smiling.

Enter Caption

Meaning

The poem 'The Nirvanic Poet' is based on the perspective of different experts. When a teacher looks out of the window, he/she sees his/her students playing. It is because that's what their first priority is. A teacher teaches students so he is more interested in looking out for his students. Similarly, a rich landlord would search for good land. If he sees a good land, he will check the land quality and profits that he'll earn. That's his priority. A florist looking out of the window would absolutely notice the blooming flowers across the garden. It's his business and first priority.

In contrast, A poet. When a poet looks out of the window, she sees heaven. She sees her whole world. A poet has the eye of an eagle. Sharp yet observative. Everything present in that surrounding is important for that poet. She will notice the children just like the teacher, she will notice the good land just like the landlord, she will also notice the blooming flowers just like the florist. Why? Because a hungry mind seeks for knowledge rather than priority. Have the wit of a poet and you'll see the difference. the casual yet intriguing way of receiving knowledge would amaze you.

10. Tenacity

It takes salt and water
for us human beings to stay alive
God provided us with both in our tears
throughout our life
Our sweat also contains salt and water
Let's not waste our time by crying harder
Instead let's drop a sweat and fulfil our desires
the desires that would make us healthy and wealthy like a
burning fire

Tenacity

Meaning

The poem 'tenacity' is exactly based on the theme of stubbornness related to one's goals and achievements. Tenacity refers to the quality displayed by someone, who just wouldn't quit even after many failed attempts. The amount of desire and determination in a person filled with tenacity... is huge and admirable. Salt and water are an important source for our well-being and survival. God has provided us with both in our tears. But if we think smartly, God had also provided us both in our sweat.

Instead of crying over our problem, we should sweat it out. Instead of crying over who insulted you, work hard! Work hard and prove them wrong! It's in us, who can show people how capable we are of achieving whatever we want. God has given us all the abilities and minds to work ourselves out. Sitting back and crying while regretting your decision won't pay your bills. Only hard work and determination will.

Get up and work hard.

The End

Here comes the end of our 'Majestic Dreamscape' Journey.

I hope you all liked the book and recieved some or the other knowledge.

If you want to share any ideas regarding further poetries, kindly send a message on the instagram account-

@the_elysianistic_art

Thank you so much for your precious time.

"All the best."

www.ingramcontent.com/pod-product-compliance
Lightning Source LLC
Chambersburg PA
CBHW021143130726
47988CB00003B/1446